INFOMOJIS

CONTINENTS

First published in paperback in
Great Britain in 2021 by Wayland
Copyright © Hodder and Stoughton, 2018
All rights reserved

Editor: Amy Pimperton
Produced by Tall Tree Ltd
Editor: Jon Richards
Designer: Ed Simkins

ISBN: 978 1 5263 0694 4

Wayland
An imprint of Hachette Children's Group
Part of Hodder and Stoughton
Carmelite House
50 Victoria Embankment
London EC4Y 0DZ

An Hachette UK Company
www.hachette.co.uk
www.hachettechildrens.co.uk

Printed and bound in Dubai

MIX
Paper from
responsible sources
FSC® C104740
FSC
www.fsc.org

This book uses different units to measure different things:
Distance is measured in metres (m) and kilometres (km).
Area is measured in square kilometres (square km).
The number of people in a given area is known as the population density, and this
is measured in people per square kilometre.
Volume is measured using cubic metres (cubic m).
The amount of rain that falls is measured in millimetres (mm) per year.
Temperature is measured in degrees Celsius (°C).
A country's wealth is measured by its Gross Domestic Product (GDP) in US dollars.

THE WORLD'S CONTINENTS

The world is divided into seven large landmasses, called continents. These are North America, South America, Europe, Africa, Asia, Oceania and Antarctica.

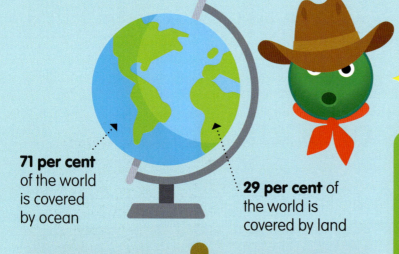

71 per cent of the world is covered by ocean

29 per cent of the world is covered by land

How many countries are there?

There are **193 members** of the United Nations, plus two observer states – Vatican City and the State of Palestine. There are also another six partially recognised states – Taiwan, Western Sahara, Kosovo, South Ossetia, Abkhazia and Northern Cyprus.

Seven continents

North America – 23 countries

Europe – 44 countries

Asia – 48 countries

Arctic Ocean

Pacific Ocean

Atlantic Ocean

Pacific Ocean

South America – 12 countries

Africa – 54 countries

Indian Ocean

Oceania – 14 countries

Southern Ocean

Antarctica 0 countries

206 nations take part in the Olympic Games.

211 nations compete in the football World Cup.

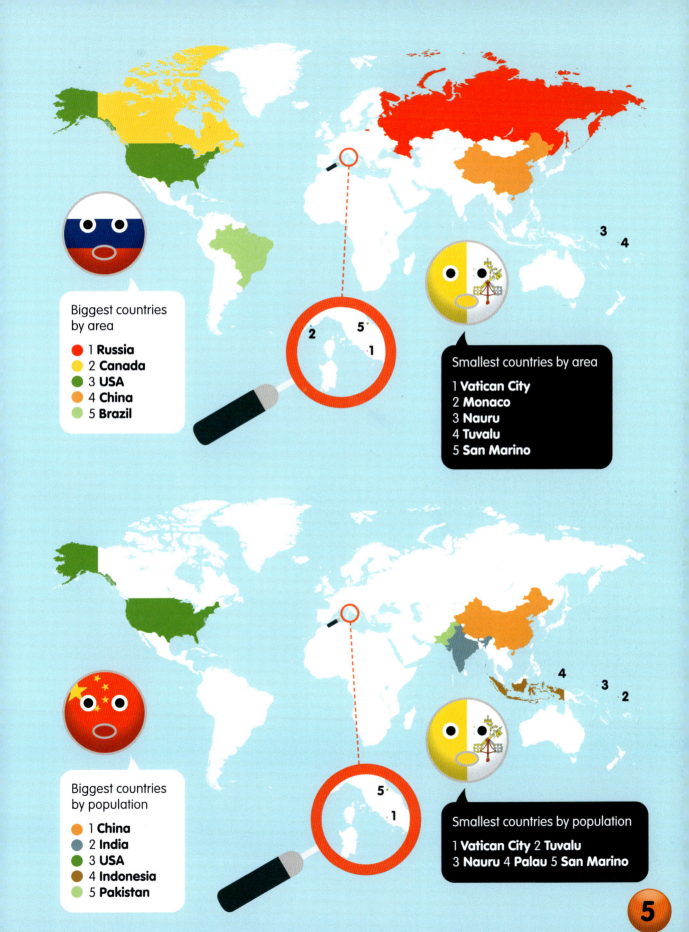

Biggest countries by area

- 1 **Russia**
- 2 **Canada**
- 3 **USA**
- 4 **China**
- 5 **Brazil**

Smallest countries by area

1 **Vatican City**
2 **Monaco**
3 **Nauru**
4 **Tuvalu**
5 **San Marino**

Biggest countries by population

- 1 **China**
- 2 **India**
- 3 **USA**
- 4 **Indonesia**
- 5 **Pakistan**

Smallest countries by population

1 **Vatican City** 2 **Tuvalu**
3 **Nauru** 4 **Palau** 5 **San Marino**

5

NORTH AMERICA, CENTRAL AMERICA AND THE CARIBBEAN

From the icy tundra in the north to the paradise islands of the Caribbean, this region is home to some of the most diverse ecosystems on the planet.

Grand Canyon

Hope you've got a head for heights! At some points, the Grand Canyon is nearly 1,900 m deep! Carved out by the mighty Colorado River, it stretches for almost 450 km and is up to 30 km wide.

Grand Canyon

Hold onto your hats!

Hurricane season
Between June and November, powerful storms, called hurricanes, form out in the Atlantic, many of which head towards the Caribbean and North America. On average, there are about six hurricanes every year.

The Caribbean

Islands of the Caribbean
The Caribbean contains more than 7,000 islands, small islets and reefs.

Rocky Mountains
Stretching for about 4,800 km, the Rocky Mountains run from northern Canada to the very south of the United States.

Denali
Soaring up to 6,190 m, Denali in Alaska is the tallest peak in North America.

Mississippi/Missouri
The Mississippi/Missouri river system is the biggest in the United States and drains 41 per cent of the country – that's a lot of water.

Great Lakes
These five huge lakes contain more than 20 per cent of the world's surface fresh water, making them the largest lake system on the planet. Lake Superior is the second-largest lake on Earth.

Great Plains
The interior of North America is dominated by a large area of grasslands called the Great Plains, covering about 1.3 million square km.

Prairies

The Great plains once supported huge herds of American Bison that numbered about 20–30 million. Hunting cut their numbers to about 1,000 by the late 19th century. Protection and careful management have seen their numbers rise to about 500,000 today.

THE COUNTRIES OF NORTH AMERICA

North America has 23 independent countries that are home to nearly 560 million people, or about 7.5 per cent of the world's total population.

Humans arrived in North America almost 25,000 years ago. They migrated from Siberia across a land bridge exposed by lower sea levels during the last ice age. They followed herds of prehistoric creatures, such as mammoths.

Alaska **(USA)**

TO SIBERIA

Biggest countries by population
1 United States – 327 million
2 Mexico – 126 million
3 Canada – 37 million
4 Guatemala – 17 million
5 Cuba – 11 million

The United States is the world's richest country, creating a Gross Domestic Product (GDP) of about US$20.2 trillion. The next richest is China with a GDP of US$13.1 trillion.

Hawaii is the youngest state of the USA, having joined the country on 21 August 1959. Today, the islands are home to more than 1.4 million people.

Hawaii **(USA)**

Mexico City is one of the largest cities in the world. The population of the Greater Mexico City conurbation is about 23.6 million people.

Canada is the world's second-largest country by area. The United States and Canada share the world's longest land border, which stretches for 8,893 km.

GREENLAND

CANADA

Land border

Great Lakes

Greenland has one of the lowest population densities in the world with only about 0.028 people per square km.

UNITED STATES OF AMERICA

Before 1914, the only way to sail from the Atlantic to the Pacific was around the dangerous Cape Horn, where powerful storms sank many ships. The opening of the **Panama Canal** in 1914 cut weeks off the journey. The canal is 77 km long. About 1,000 ships used the canal in its first year. Today, nearly 15,000 ships sail through it every year.

Panama Canal route

Cape Horn route

BAHAMAS

ST KITTS AND NEVIS

MEXICO

DOMINICAN REPUBLIC

PUERTO RICO

ANTIGUA AND BARBUDA

CUBA

HONDURAS

BELIZE

JAMAICA

HAITI

ST LUCIA

DOMINICA

NICARAGUA

GRENADA

BARBADOS

EL SALVADOR

PANAMA

ST VINCENT AND THE GRENADINES

GUATEMALA

COSTA RICA

TRINIDAD AND TOBAGO

SOUTH AMERICA

This continent contains lush rainforests, cold, dry deserts, mighty rivers and towering, ice-covered peaks.

Rainforest
Tropical rainforests don't get bigger than the Amazonian rainforest. It covers about 5.5 million square km – about 60 per cent of the size of the USA.

Slovenian swimmer Martin Strel completed a marathon swim of the Amazon River in 2007, covering the 6,400 km in just 66 days.

Amazon River
It may not be the longest river in the world, but the Amazon is the mightiest. It drains an area of more than 7 million square km and empties about 210,000 cubic m of water into the ocean every single second – that's the same volume as 85 Olympic swimming pools – EVERY SINGLE SECOND!

Angel Falls

Amazon River

The plants of the rainforest produce a huge amount of oxygen, which is vital to life. Some calculations estimate that it produces 20 per cent of the world's oxygen.

The Amazonian rainforest is home to 40,000 plant species, 1,300 bird species, 3,000 types of fish, 430 species of mammal, and more than 100,000 species of invertebrate.

The leaves on the rainforest canopy are so thick that when it rains it can take 10 minutes for the water to reach the ground.

Watch out for piranhas!

THE ANDES

Andes
The Andes are the longest chain of land mountains on the planet, stretching for 7,000 km down the length of the continent. The tallest peak is Aconcagua at 6,962 m high.

ATACAMA DESERT

Aconcagua

Angel Falls
The tallest falls in the world with a single plunge of 807 m.

Atacama Desert
Located in Chile (see page 13), the Atacama Desert is one of the driest places on the planet with an average rainfall of just 15 mm a year. Some parts receive only 1 mm a year.

THE COUNTRIES OF SOUTH AMERICA

South America's 12 countries are spread across 17.8 million square km and are home to about 423.5 million people.

Biggest countries by population

1 Brazil – 209 million
2 Colombia – 49 million
3 Argentina – 44 million
4 Peru – 31 million
5 Venezuela – 28 million

The Amazon rainforest (see page 11) is home to up to 500 different Amerindian tribes. About 50 of these have not had any contact with the outside world.

We sloths just love hanging around!

La Rinconada, Peru is the highest city in the world, at an altitude of 5,130 metres. It is home to more than 50,000 people.

FRENCH GUIANA

SURINAME

GUYANA

VENEZUELA

COLOMBIA

BRAZIL

ECUADOR

PERU

La Rinconada

The largest city in South America is São Paulo, Brazil, with more than 21 million people – that's almost seven times the population of Uruguay.

Running from the top of Alaska right down to Ushuaia at the southern tip of Argentina, the Pan-American Highway is about 30,000 km long. It's the world's longest drivable road.

São Paulo

Beep! Beep!

Falkland Islands

URUGUAY

PARAGUAY

BOLIVIA

ARGENTINA

CHILE

Hydropower
99.9% of Paraguay's electricity is hydroelectric, compared to a world average of about 16.5%.

99.9%

16.5%

Smallest countries by population
1 French Guiana – 275,000
2 Suriname – 575,000
3 Guyana – 778,000
4 Uruguay – 3.4 million
5 Paraguay – 7 million

EUROPE

Europe stretches from the chilly Arctic Ocean in the north to the warm shores of the Mediterranean in the south. It may be a diverse continent, but it is one of the smallest continents on the planet, making up less than 7 per cent of the land area.

Key mountain ranges

Mountain range

Mount Narodnaya

Ural Mountains

Mont Blanc

Danube

Alps

Mount Elbrus

Pyrenees

Black Sea

Caspian Sea

Aneto

Mount Etna

Caucasus Mountains

Mediterranean

Pyrenees – separating the countries of France and Spain, this chain stretches from the Atlantic to the Mediterranean. Its highest peak is **Aneto** at 3,404 m tall.

Alps – found in central western Europe, this mountain chain stretches for 1,200 km. Its highest point is **Mont Blanc** at 4,809 m tall, but it has more than 100 mountains that are taller than 4,000 m.

Islands of Greece
The country of Greece is made up of more than 6,000 islands, but only about 200 of these are inhabited.

Greece

14

Rugged coast
With its jagged bays and fjords, the coastline of Norway measures about 100,000 km – long enough to stretch around the world two-and-a-half times!

Mount Etna on the island of Sicily is one of the most active volcanoes on Earth. Its peak is at about 3,330 m, but this can vary with eruptions.

Temperature range
Average winter temperatures in Moscow, Russia – -10°C

Average summer temperatures in Cordoba, Spain – 36.4°C

Brrrrrrrrrrrr!

Caucasus Mountains – this chain of mountains runs from the Black Sea to the Caspian Sea.

Located in the **Caucasus**, **Mount Elbrus** is the highest point in Europe. This extinct volcano is 5,642 m high.

Ural Mountains – this huge chain of mountains runs north to south for about 2,500 km through the centre of Russia. Its tallest point is **Mount Narodnaya** at 1,895 m tall.

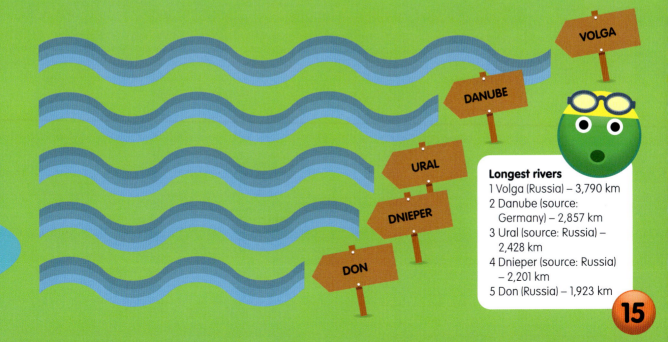

VOLGA

DANUBE

URAL

DNIEPER

DON

Longest rivers
1 Volga (Russia) – 3,790 km
2 Danube (source: Germany) – 2,857 km
3 Ural (source: Russia) – 2,428 km
4 Dnieper (source: Russia) – 2,201 km
5 Don (Russia) – 1,923 km

THE COUNTRIES OF EUROPE

About 746 million people live in some 44 countries that make up Europe, accounting for about 11 per cent of the world's population.

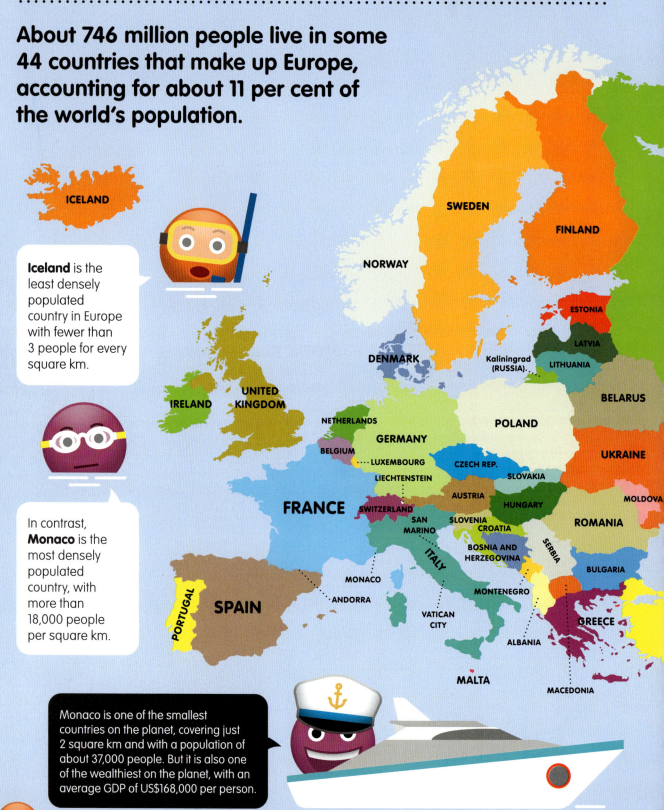

Iceland is the least densely populated country in Europe with fewer than 3 people for every square km.

In contrast, **Monaco** is the most densely populated country, with more than 18,000 people per square km.

Monaco is one of the smallest countries on the planet, covering just 2 square km and with a population of about 37,000 people. But it is also one of the wealthiest on the planet, with an average GDP of US$168,000 per person.

ICELAND
SWEDEN
FINLAND
NORWAY
ESTONIA
LATVIA
LITHUANIA
DENMARK
Kaliningrad (RUSSIA)
BELARUS
IRELAND
UNITED KINGDOM
NETHERLANDS
GERMANY
POLAND
BELGIUM
LUXEMBOURG
CZECH REP.
SLOVAKIA
UKRAINE
LIECHTENSTEIN
AUSTRIA
HUNGARY
MOLDOVA
FRANCE
SWITZERLAND
SAN MARINO
SLOVENIA
CROATIA
ROMANIA
SERBIA
BOSNIA AND HERZEGOVINA
BULGARIA
PORTUGAL
SPAIN
MONACO
ANDORRA
ITALY
MONTENEGRO
GREECE
VATICAN CITY
ALBANIA
MALTA
MACEDONIA

RUSSIA

EUROPE

ASIA

RUSSIA

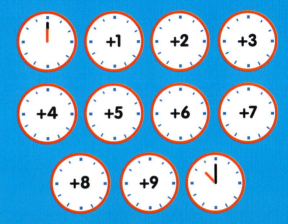

Russia is the largest country in the world, making up nearly 40 per cent of the continent's area. It covers an area of 17,098,242 square km and has 11 different time zones. So when it's 12 a.m. in Kaliningrad in the west, it's 10 a.m. in Kamchatka in the far east.

+1	+2	+3
+4	+5	+6	+7
+8	+9	

Biggest countries by population
1 Russia – 145 million
2 Turkey – 83.6 million
3 Germany – 83.1 million
4 France – 67.4 million
5 UK – 67.1 million

Smallest countries by population
1 Vatican City – 799
2 San Marino – 33,000
3 Liechtenstein – 37,000
4 Monaco – 38,000
5 Andorra – 77,000

TURKEY

CYPRUS

Shrinking population
100 years ago, Europe had about one-quarter of the world's population. Today, it has about one-ninth. It is predicted that, by 2050, it will only be home to about one-fifteenth of the world's people.

AFRICA

With scorching deserts, soaring mountains, powerful rivers and lush grasslands, Africa is a continent of extremes.

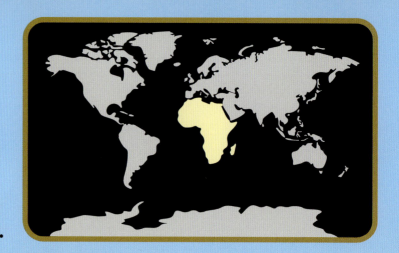

Longest river
The Nile is one epic river. It's the longest river in the world stretching for 6,583 km from the centre of Africa up to the Mediterranean.

Sahara
Dominating northern Africa, the Sahara is the world's biggest hot desert. It covers 9,200,000 square km – the same area as China.

SAHARA

Great Green Wall
Plans are in action to create a 'wall' of trees running for 8,000 km across the Sahel, on the southern edge of the Sahara. Millions of trees are being planted to stop the spread of the Sahara.

The Skeleton Coast
The seashore of Namibia and southern Angola is known as the Skeleton Coast after all the whale and seal bones that were washed up on the beaches. Today, there are also the remains of more than 1,000 shipwrecks littering the coast.

Kilimanjaro

Towering above the African grasslands, Kilimanjaro is the tallest mountain in Africa at 5,895 metres tall. It's actually made up of three volcanoes – two of these are extinct, but one is only dormant and could still erupt!

KILIMANJARO

THE NILE

Lemur

Madagascar

As an island, the wildlife of Madagascar has evolved in isolation and about 90 per cent of the plants and animals are only found there, including lemurs.

Madagascar

Cradle of life

Some time between 350,000 and 260,000 years ago, modern humans, *Homo sapiens*, evolved in central Africa before spreading throughout the world.

Let me know if you spot a lion!

African Savanna

The African tropical grasslands are called the savanna. These rich grasslands support huge herds of zebras, wildebeest and antelopes as well as hunters such as lions.

19

THE COUNTRIES OF AFRICA

More than 1.2 billion people live in Africa. The continent covers nearly 30.5 million square km, making it the second-largest in terms of both area and population.

Algeria is the largest country in Africa by area, covering about 2.4 million square km, or about 8 per cent of the continent.

Biggest countries by population
1 Nigeria – 206 million
2 Ethiopia – 109 million
3 Democratic Republic of the Congo – 102 million
4 Egypt – 101 million
5 South Africa – 59 million

The largest city in Africa is Lagos, Nigeria, which is home to about 17.6 million people.

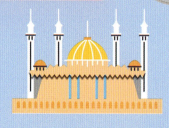

The people of Africa speak more than 2,000 languages (and it may be as many as 3,000), and Nigeria has more than 500 languages alone. Arabic is the most widely used, with about 150,000,000 speakers.

Smallest countries by population
1 Seychelles – 90,000
2 São Tomé and Príncipe – 201,000
3 Cape Verde – 491,000
4 Western Sahara – 510,000
5 Comoros – 806,000

Home to more than 1.2 billion people (16 per cent of the world's population), Africa's population is set to rise to 2.3 billion people by 2050, making it the fastest growing continent on the planet.

The tiniest country in Africa is the **Seychelles**, which has an area of just 451 square km – that's just three-quarters the area of Chicago (or just a bit bigger than the Isle of Wight).

EGYPT

CHAD

SUDAN

ERITREA

DJIBOUTI

ETHIOPIA

CENTRAL AFRICAN REPUBLIC

SOUTH SUDAN

SOMALIA

UGANDA

KENYA

DEMOCRATIC REPUBLIC OF THE CONGO

RWANDA

BURUNDI

TANZANIA

SEYCHELLES

COMOROS

MALAWI

ZAMBIA

MOZAMBIQUE

MADAGASCAR

ZIMBABWE

BOTSWANA

Africa's biggest cities:
Lagos, Nigeria – 21 million people
Cairo, Egypt – 20 million people
Kinshasa-Brazzaville, Democratic Republic of the Congo and Republic of the Congo – 16 million people
Gauteng, South Africa – 14 million people

LESOTHO

SWAZILAND

SOUTH AFRICA

21

ASIA

Everything about Asia is big. It's the biggest continent, has the biggest mountains, has the most people and has the biggest countries by population.

Mount Everest is the highest peak on the planet, with a summit at 8,848 m above sea level. It was first climbed in 1953 by Tenzing Norgay from Nepal and Edmund Hillary from New Zealand.

MOUNT EVEREST

The Himalayas

Separating the rest of Asia from India, the Himalayas is the highest mountain chain in the world. It has ten peaks that are taller than 8,000 m. The air above this height is too thin to sustain life, that's why it's called the 'death zone'.

Steppes

The centre of Asia has a huge area of temperate grassland called the Steppes.

The Empty Quarter

The Rub' al Khali, or 'Empty Quarter', in the Arabian Peninsula is the biggest area of sand desert in the world. This huge area of sand covers about 650,000 square km – bigger than the state of California.

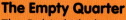

RUB' AL KHALI

The country of **Indonesia** is made up of nearly 13,500 islands, stretching in a huge chain, or archipelago, that is more than 5,000 km long.

INDONESIA

Deforestation
Between 1990 and 2010, Southeast Asia's forests shrank by about 330,000 square km due to the global demand for timber, paper, palm oil and other products. That's bigger than the whole of Vietnam!

Care for a dip?

GOBI DESERT

LAKE BAIKAL

Gobi Desert
Covering nearly 1.3 million square km, the Gobi Desert is a large cold desert in the heart of Asia. Temperatures can plummet to -43°C.

Lake Baikal
This vast body of water is the biggest by volume in the world. It holds about 23 per cent of the world's surface fresh water. It's also the world's deepest lake, with a depth of up to 1,642 m – that's twice the height of the Burj Khalifa, the world's tallest building.

It is home to many unique species of animals, including the Baikal seal.

THE COUNTRIES OF ASIA

There are nearly 50 countries in Asia, and they're home to nearly 4.5 billion people – that's nearly two-thirds of the world's population.

Biggest countries by population
1 China – 1,400 million
2 India – 1,300 million
3 Indonesia – 255 million
4 Pakistan – 202 million
5 Bangladesh – 159 million

India is the world's largest producer of movies, making more than 2,500 films every year. The Indian film industry is known as Bollywood.

Asia is the continent where some of the earliest civilisations flourished.

Mesopotamia
('land between rivers')
3500 BCE–500 BCE
Location – modern-day Iran, Syria and Turkey

Indus Valley Civilisation
2600 BCE–1700 BCE
Location – around the Indus River, northern Pakistan, Afghanistan and north west India

The Maldives is threatened by rising sea levels – caused by global warming – more than any other country on Earth. The whole country is less than 2.5 m above sea level.

EUROPE

ASIA

KAZAKHSTAN

GEORGIA

AZERBAIJAN

ARMENIA

UZBEKISTAN

KYRGYZSTAN

TURKMENISTAN

TAJIKISTAN

TURKEY

SYRIA

LEBANON

IRAQ

KUWAIT

IRAN

AFGHANISTAN

PAKISTAN

NEPA

Delhi

PALESTINE

QATAR

ISRAEL

BAHRAIN

UAE

Karachi

JORDAN

SAUDI ARABIA

OMAN

INDIA

YEMEN

SRI LANKA

MALDIVES

RUSSIA

MONGOLIA

CHINA

Smallest countries by population
1 Brunei – 421,000
2 Maldives – 557,000
3 Bhutan – 760,000
4 Bahrain – 1.3 million
5 Timor-Leste – 1.6 million

Asia is home to the biggest city populations on the planet:
1 Tokyo, Japan – 40.4 million
2 Jakarta, Indonesia – 31.3 million
3 Delhi, India – 30.3 million
4 Mumbai, India – 25.1 million

NORTH
KOREA

Tokyo

JAPAN

SOUTH
KOREA

Some economists predict that China's economy will overtake the United States' to become the biggest in the world by 2030.

BHUTAN

BANGLADESH

LAOS

MYANMAR

THAILAND   VIETNAM

PHILIPPINES

CAMBODIA   BRUNEI

MALAYSIA

INDONESIA

Jakarta

TIMOR-LESTE

The nation of Timor-Leste is one of the youngest countries on the planet. It declared independence from Indonesia and became a sovereign state on 20 May 2002.

OCEANIA

This continent may span a vast region across the southern Pacific, but it's the smallest continent in terms of land area and is the continent with the second lowest population, after Antarctica.

GUAM (USA)

PALAU

MICRONESIA

ASIA

PAPUA NEW GUINEA

SOLOMON ISLANDS

Australia is the driest inhabited continent with an average annual rainfall of just 500 mm over the entire country.

It has a population density of less than 3 people per square km – one of the lowest on the planet.

AUSTRALIA

Biggest countries by population
1 Australia – 25.5 million
2 Papua New Guinea – 8.9 million
3 New Zealand – 4.8 million
4 Fiji – 896,000
5 Solomon Islands – 686,000

MARSHALL ISLANDS

Oceania is home to just 40 million people, about 0.55 per cent of the world's total. More than half of these live in Australia (23.8 million).

Oceania's total land area is about 8.5 million square km – about the same area as Brazil. About 7.7 million square km of this is made up of Australia.

KIRIBATI

NAURU

TUVALU

TOKELAU (NEW ZEALAND)

SAMOA

COOK ISLANDS (NEW ZEALAND)

VANUATU

AMERICAN SAMOA (USA)

FIJI

TONGA

FRENCH POLYNESIA (FRANCE).

NEW CALEDONIA (FRANCE)

There are more than 10,000 islands scattered throughout Oceania.

New Zealand facts

In 1883, **New Zealand** became the first country to give the vote to women.

The highest peak on New Zealand is Aoraki (Mount Cook), with a summit at 3,724 m.

NEW ZEALAND

Nearly one-third of New Zealand is covered by forest.

ANTARCTICA

This frozen region is the coldest, driest and windiest continent on the planet and is so hostile that it has no permanent inhabitants. It is the world's last great wilderness.

TO SOUTH AMERICA

About 98 per cent of the continent's 14 million square km is covered by a thick ice sheet.

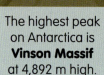

The highest peak on Antarctica is **Vinson Massif** at 4,892 m high.

The ice sheet has an average thickness of 1.9 km. The continent holds 90 per cent of the world's ice and 70 per cent of all its fresh water.

Even though it's covered in frozen water, Antarctica is technically a desert as it has an annual precipitation of just 200 mm.

TO AFRICA

On 7 January 1978, Argentine Emilio Marcos Palma became the first person to be born in Antarctica.

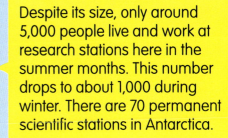
Despite its size, only around 5,000 people live and work at research stations here in the summer months. This number drops to about 1,000 during winter. There are 70 permanent scientific stations in Antarctica.

The continent is governed by the Antarctic Treaty System which prohibits any military activity and mining.

-89.2°C – the lowest-ever recorded temperature on Earth was at Vostok Station, Antarctica.

VOSTOK STATION

TO AUSTRALIA

Vostok is Antarctica's largest lake and one of the biggest sub-glacial lakes on the planet. It's actually located about 4,000 m beneath the surface of the ice and covers an area of about 12,500 square km.

Vostok Station

Ice sheet

Lake Vostok

GLOSSARY

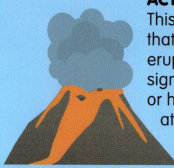

ACTIVE VOLCANO
This is a volcano that is currently erupting, showing signs of erupting, or has erupted at least once in the last 10,000 years.

ALTITUDE
The height of an object. It is usually given as a height above sea level.

ARCHIPELAGO
The name given to a long chain of small islands.

CANOPY
The layer of leaves and branches that forms at the top of a forest. It is the highest level of the forest, with only a few emergent trees standing taller than this level.

CONTINENT
A very large area of land. Earth has seven continents, including North America, South America, Europe, Africa, Asia, Oceania and Antarctica.

COUNTRY
An area or region that usually has its own government.

DEFORESTATION
To remove large numbers of trees and clear areas of forest.

DORMANT VOLCANO
This is a volcano that is not erupting at the moment, and isn't showing signs that it will erupt, but has erupted at least once in the last 10,000 years and could still erupt at any moment.

EXTINCT VOLCANO
This is a volcano that has not erupted for at least 10,000 years and is not expected to erupt again.

FJORD
A steep-sided gorge that runs inland from the sea. Carved by glaciers thousands of years ago, fjords are most common on the coast of Norway.

GLOBAL WARMING
This is the gradual rise in Earth's temperatures, which scientists believe is due to increased levels of greenhouse gases, such as carbon dioxide and methane.

GROSS DOMESTIC PRODUCT
Also known as GDP, this is the total amount of goods and services that a country has provided over a year.

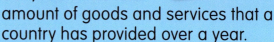

HERD
The name given to a large group of animals that live together.

HURRICANE
The name given to a tropical cyclone that forms over the Atlantic or the